Microsoft Project 2016 Keyboard Shortcuts

For Windows

By

U. C-Abel Books.

All Rights Reserved

First Edition: 2016

Copyright @ U. C-Abel Books. ISBN-13: 978-1533630100

ISBN-13: 978-1533630100
ISBN-10: 1533630100

Published by U. C-Abel Books.

Table of Contents

Acknowledgement.

U. C-Abel Books will not take all the credits for Microsoft Project 2016 keyboard shortcuts listed in this book, but shares it with Microsoft Corporation because some of the shortcut keys came from them and are "used with permission from Microsoft".

Dedication

This book is dedicated to computer users and lovers of keyboard shortcuts all over the world.

Introduction.

We enjoy using shortcut keys because they set us on a high plane that astonishes people around us when we work with them. As wonderful shortcuts users, the worst eyesore we witness in computing is to see somebody sluggishly struggling to execute a task through mouse usage when in actual sense shortcuts will help to save that person the time wasted. Most people have asked us to help them with a list of shortcut keys that can make them work as smartly as we do and that drove us into research to broaden our knowledge and truly help them as they demanded, that is the reason for the existence of this book. It is a great tool for lovers of shortcuts, and those who want to join the group.

Most times, the things we love don't come by easily. It is our love for keyboard shortcuts that made us to bear long sleepless nights like owls, just to make sure we get the best out of it, and it is the best we got that we are sharing with you in this book. You cannot be the same at computing after reading this book. The time you entrusted to our care is an expensive possession and we promise not to mess it up.

Thank you.

What to Know Before You Begin.

General Notes.

1. It is important to note that when using shortcuts to perform any command, you should make sure the target area is active, if not, you may get a wrong result. Example, if you want to highlight all texts, you must make sure the text field is active and if an object, make sure the object area is active. The active area is always known by the location where the cursor of your computer blinks.

2. Most of the keyboard shortcuts you will see in this book refer to the U.S. keyboard layout. Keys for other layouts might not correspond exactly to the keys on a U.S. keyboard.

3. The plus (+) signs that come in the middle of keyboard shortcuts simply mean the keys are meant to be combined or held down together not to be added as one of the shortcut keys. In a case where plus sign is needed; it will be duplicated (++).

4. For keyboard shortcuts in which you press one key immediately followed by another key, the keys are separated by a comma (,).

5. It is also important to note that the shortcut keys listed in this book are for Microsoft Project 2016.

Short Forms Used in This Book and Their Full Meaning.

The following are short forms of keyboard shortcuts used in this Microsoft Project 2016 Keyboard Shortcuts book and their full meaning.

1. Alt   -   Alternate Key
2. Caps Lock -   Caps Lock Key
3. Ctrl   -   Control Key
4. Esc   -   Escape Key
5. F   -   Function Key
6. Num Lock   -   Number Lock Key
7. Shft   -   Shift Key
8. Tab   -   Tabulate Key
9. Win   -   Windows logo key
10. Prt sc   -   Print Screen

CHAPTER 1.

Gathering The Basic Knowledge Of Keyboard Shortcuts.

Without the existence of the keyboard, there wouldn't have been anything like keyboard shortcuts, so in this chapter we will learn a little about keyboard before moving to keyboard shortcuts.

1. Definition of Computer Keyboard.
This is an input device that is used to send data to the computer memory.

Sketch of a Keyboard

1.1 Types of Keyboard.

   i. Standard (Basic) Keyboard.
   ii. Enhanced (Extended) Keyboard.

i. **Standard Keyboard:** This is a keyboard designed during the 1800s for mechanical typewriters with just 10 function keys (F keys) placed at the left side of it.

ii. **Enhanced Keyboard:** This is the current 101 to 102-key keyboard that is included in almost all the personal computers (PCs) of nowadays, which has 12 function keys at the top side of it.

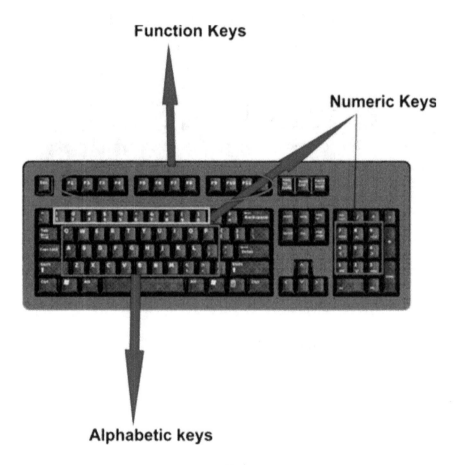

1.2 Segments of the keyboard

- Numeric keys
- Alphabetic keys
- Punctuation keys
- Windows Logo key.
- Function keys
- Special keys

Numeric Keys: Numeric keys are keys with numbers from **0 - 9**.

Alphabetic Keys: These are keys that have alphabets on them, ranging from **A-Z**.

Punctuation Keys: These are keys of the keyboard used for punctuation. Examples include comma, full stop, colon, question marks, hyphen etc.

Windows Logo Key: A key on Microsoft Computer keyboard with its logo displayed on it. Search for this 🚩 on your keyboard.

Function Keys: These are keys that have **F** on them which are usually combined with other keys. They are F1 - F12, and are also in the class called Special Keys.

Special Keys: These are keys that perform special functions. They include: Tab, Ctrl, Caps lock, Insert,

Prt sc, alt gr, Shift, Home, Num lock, Esc and many others. Special keys work according to the type of computer involved. In some keyboard layout, especially laptops, the keys that turn the speaker on/off, the one that increases/decreases volume, the key that turns the computer Wifi on/off are also special keys.

Other Special Keys Worthy of Note.

Enter Key: This is located at the right-hand corner of the keyboard. It is used to send messages to the computer to execute commands, in most cases it is used to mean "Ok" or "Go".

Escape Key (ESC): This is the first key on the upper left of the keyboard. It is used to cancel routines, close menus and select options such as **Save** according to circumstance.

Control Key (CTRL): It is located on the bottom row of the left and right hand side of the keyboard. They also work with the function keys to execute commands using Keyboard shortcuts (key combinations).

Alternate Key (ALT): It is located on the bottom row, very close to the CTRL key on both side of the keyboard. It enables many editing functions to be accomplished by using some keystroke combinations on the keyboard.

Shift Key: This adds to the functions of the function keys. In addition, it enables the use of alternative function of a particular button (key), especially, those with more than one function on a key. E.g. use of capital letters, symbols and numbers.

1.3. Selecting/Highlighting With the Keyboard.

This is a highlighting method or style where data is selected using the keyboard instead of a computer mouse.

To do this:

- Move your cursor to the text you want to highlight, make sure that area is active,
- Hold down the shift key with one finger
- Then use another finger to move the arrow key that points to the direction you want to highlight.

1.4 The Operating Modes Of The Keyboard.

Just like the mouse the keyboard has two operating modes. The two modes are Text Entering and Command Mode.

a. **Text Entering Mode:** this mode gives the operator/user the opportunity to type text.

b.   **Command Mode:** this is used to command the operating system/software/application to execute commands in certain ways.

2. Ways To Improve In Your Typing Skill.

1. Put Your Eyes Off The Keyboard.

This is the aspect of keyboard usage that many don't find funny because they always ask. "How can I put my eyes off the keyboard when I am running away from the occurrence of errors on my file?" My aim is to be fast, is this not going to slow me down?

Of course, there will be errors and at the same time your speed will slow down but the motive behind the introduction of this method is to make you faster than you are. Looking at your keyboard while you type can make you get a sore neck, it is better you learn to touch type because the more you type with your eyes fixed on the screen instead of the keyboard, the faster you become.

An alternative to keeping your eyes off your keyboard is to use the "*Das Keyboard Ultimate*".

2. Errors Challenge You

It is better to fail than not to try at all. Not trying at all is an attribute of the weak and lazybones. When you make mistakes, try again because errors are opportunities for improvement.

3. Good Posture (Position Yourself Well).
Do not adopt an awkward position while typing. You should get everything on your desk organized or arranged before sitting to type. Your posture while typing contributes to your speed and productivity.

4. Practice
Here is the conclusion of everything said above. You have to practice your shortcuts constantly. The practice alone is a way of improvement. "Practice brings improvement". Practice always.

2.1 Software That Will Help You Improve In Your Typing Skill.

There are several Software programs for typing that both kids and adults can use for their typing skill. Here is a list of software that can help you improve in your typing: Mavis Beacon, Typing Instructor, Mucky Typing Adventure, Rapid Tying Tutor, Letter Chase Tying Tutor, Alice Touch Typing Tutor and many more. Personally, I recommend Mavis Beacon.

To learn typing with MAVIS BEACON, install Mavis Beacon software to your computer, start with keyboard lesson, then move to games. Games like **Penguin Crossing, Creature Lab** or **Space Junk** will help you become a professional in typing. Typing and keyboard shortcuts work hand-in-hand.

Sketch of a computer mouse

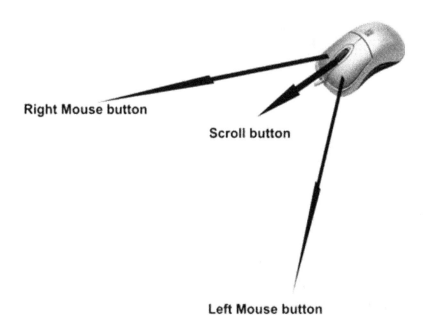

Right Mouse button

Scroll button

Left Mouse button

3. Mouse:

This is an oval-shaped portable input device with three buttons for scrolling, left clicking, and right clicking that enables work to be done effectively on a computer. The plural form of mouse is mice.

3.1 Types of Computer Mouse

- Mechanical Mouse
- Optical Mechanical Mouse (Optomechanical)
- Laser Mouse
- Optical Mouse

- BlueTrack Mouse

3.2 Forms of Clicking:

Left Clicking: This is the process of clicking the left side button of the mouse. It can be called *clicking* without the addition of *left*.

Right Clicking: It is the process of clicking the right side button of the mouse.

Double Clicking: It is the process of clicking the left side button two times (twice) and immediately.

Double clicking is used to select a word while thrice clicking is used to select a sentence or paragraph.

Scroll Button: It is the little key attached to the mouse that looks like a tiny wheel. It takes you up and down a page when moved.

3.3 Mouse Pad: This is a small soft mat that is placed under the mouse to make it have a free movement.

3.4 Laptop Mouse Touchpad

This unlike the mouse we explained above is not external, rather it is inbuilt (comes with a laptop computer). With the presence of a laptop mouse touchpad, an external mouse is not needed to use a laptop, except in a case where it is malfunctioning or the operator prefers to use external one for some reasons.

The laptop mouse touchpad is usually positioned at the end of the keyboard section of a laptop computer. It is rectangular in shape with two buttons positioned below it. The two buttons/keys are used for left and right clicking just like the external mouse. Some laptops come with four mouse keys. Two placed above the mouse for left and right clicking and two other keys placed below it for the same function.

4. Definition Of Keyboard Shortcuts.

Keyboard shortcuts are defined as a series of keys, sometimes with combination that execute tasks that typically involve the use of mouse or other input devices.

5. Why You Should Use Shortcuts.

1. One may not be able to use a computer mouse easily because of disability or pain.

2. One may not be able to see the mouse pointer as a result of vision impairment, in such case what will the person do? The answer is SHORTCUT.

3. Research has made it known that Extensive mouse usage is related to Repetitive Syndrome Injury (RSI) greatly than the use of keyboard.

4. Keyboard shortcuts speed up computer users, making learning them a worthwhile effort.

5. When performing a job that requires precision, it is wise that you use the keyboard instead of mouse, for instance, if you are dealing with Text Editing, it is better you handle it using keyboard shortcuts than spending more time with mouse alone.

6. Studies calculate that using keyboard shortcuts allows working 10 times faster than working with the mouse. The time you spend looking for the mouse and then getting the cursor to the position you want is lost! Reducing your work duration by 10 times brings you greater results.

5.1 Ways To Become A Lover Of Shortcuts.

1. Always have the urge to learn new shortcut keys associated with the programs you use.
2. Be happy whenever you learn a new shortcut.
3. Try as much as you can to apply the new shortcuts you learnt.
4. Always bear it in mind that learning new shortcuts is worth it.

5. Always remember that the use of keyboard shortcuts keeps people healthy while performing computing activities.

5.2 How To Learn New Shortcut Keys

1. Do a research for them: quick reference (a cheat sheet comprehensively compiled) can go a long way to help you improve.
2. Buy applications that show you keyboard shortcuts every time you execute an action with the mouse.
3. Disconnect your mouse if you must learn this fast.
4. Read user manuals and help topics (Whether offline or online).

5.3 Your Reward For Knowing Shortcut Keys.

1. You will get faster unimaginably.
2. Your level of efficiency will increase.
3. You will find it easy to use.
4. Opportunities are high that you will become an expert in what you do.
5. You won't have to go for **Office button**, click **New,** click **Blank and Recent** and click **Create** just to insert a fresh/blank page. **Ctrl +N** takes care of that in a second.

A Funny Note: Keyboard Shortcuts and Mousing are in a marital union with Keyboard Shortcuts being the head and it will be unfair for anybody to put asunder between them.

5.4 Why We Emphasize On The Use of Shortcuts.

You may never ditch your mouse completely unless you are ready to make your brain a box of keyboard shortcuts which will really be frustrating. Just imagine yourself learning all the shortcuts for the programs you use and its various versions. You shouldn't learn keyboard shortcuts that way.

Why we are emphasizing on the use of shortcuts is because mouse usage is becoming unusually common and unhealthy, too. So we just want to make sure both are combined so you can get fast, productive and healthy in your computing activities. All you need to know is just the most important ones associated with the programs you use.

CHAPTER 2.

15 (Fifteen) Special Keyboard Shortcuts.

The fifteen special keyboard shortcuts are fifteen (15) shortcut keys every computer user should know.

The following table contains the list of keyboard shortcuts every computer user should know.

1. **Ctrl + A:** Control plus A, highlights or selects everything you have in the environment where you are working.

    > *If you are like **"Wow, the content of this document is large and there is no time to select all of it, besides, it's going to mount pressure on my computer?"** Using the mouse for this is an outdated method of handling a task like selecting all, Ctrl+A will take care of that within seconds.*

2. **Ctrl + C:** Control plus C copies any highlighted or selected element within the work environment.

    > *Saves the time and stress which would have been used to right click and click again just to copy. Use ctrl+c.*

3. **Ctrl + N:** Control plus N opens a new window.
Instead of clicking **File, New, blank/ template** *and another* **click,** *just press* **Ctrl + N** *and a fresh window will appear instantly.*

4. **Ctrl + O:** Control plus O opens a new program.
Use ctrl +O when you want to locate or open a file or program.

5. **Ctrl + P:** Control plus P prints the active document.
Always use this to locate the printer dialog box and print.

6. **Ctrl + S:** Control plus S saves a new document or file and changes made by the user.
Going for the mouse? Please stop! Don't use the mouse. Just press Ctrl+S and everything will be saved.

7. **Ctrl +V:** Control plus V pastes copied elements into the active area of the program in use.
Using ctrl+V in a case like this Saves the time and stress of right clicking and clicking again just to paste.

8. **Ctrl + W:** Control plus W is used to close the page you are working on when you want to leave the work environment.

> *"There is a way Peace does this without using the mouse. Oh my God, why didn't I learn it then?"* Don't worry, I have the answer, Peace presses Ctrl+W to close active windows.

9. **Ctrl + X:** Control plus X cuts elements (making the elements to disappear from their original place). The difference between cutting and deleting elements is that in Cutting, what was cut doesn't get lost permanently but prepares itself so that it can be pasted in another location selected by the user.

> *Use ctrl+x when you think **"this shouldn't be here and I can't stand the stress of retyping or redesigning it in the rightful place it belongs".***

10. **Ctrl + Y:** Control plus Y redoes an undone action.

> *Ctrl+Z brought back what you didn't need? Press Ctrl+ Y to remove it again.*

11. **Ctrl + Z:** Control plus Z undoes actions.

Can't find what you typed now or a picture you inserted, it suddenly disappeared or you mistakenly removed it? Press Ctrl+Z to bring it back.

12. **Alt + F4:** Alternative plus F4 closes active windows or items.

   *You don't need to move the mouse in order to close an active window, just press **Alt + F4** if you are done or don't want somebody who is coming to see what you are doing.*

13. **Ctrl + F6:** Control plus F6 Navigates between open windows, making it possible for a user to see what is happening in windows that are active.
   Are you working in Microsoft Word and want to find out if the other active window where your browser is loading a page is still progressing? Use Ctrl + F6.

14. **F1:** This displays the help window.

   *Is your computer malfunctioning? Use **F1** to find help when you don't know what next to do.*

15. **F12:** This enables user to make changes to an already saved document.

F12 is the shortcut to use when you want to change the format in which you saved your existing document, password it, change its name, change the file location or destination, or make other changes to it. It will save your time.

CHAPTER 3.

Keyboard Shortcuts In Project 2016.

Definition of Program: Microsoft Project is a project management software, developed and sold by Microsoft that helps users to create schedules, distribute resources and manage budgets.

The following list contains keyboard shortcuts that will boost your productivity in Microsoft Project.

Microsoft Office Basics

Keyboard access to the ribbon and Tell me

1. Press Alt.

   The KeyTips are displayed over each feature that is available in the current view.

2. Press the letter that appears in the KeyTip over the feature that you want to use.

   Tip: Press Q to look up a command or search for a Help topic.

3. Depending on which letter you press, additional KeyTips may appear. For example, if the **Home**

tab is active and you press W, the **View** tab is displayed, along with the KeyTips for the groups on that tab.

4. Continue pressing letters until you press the letter of the command or control that you want to use. In some cases, you must first press the letter of the group that contains the command.

Note: To cancel the action that you are taking and hide the KeyTips, press Alt.

Display and use windows

TASK	SHORTCUT
Switch to the next window.	Alt+Tab
Switch to the previous window.	Alt+Shift+Tab
Close the active window.	Ctrl+W or Ctrl+F4
Restore the size of the active window after you maximize it.	Ctrl+F5
Move to a task pane from another pane in the program window (clockwise direction). You may need to press F6 more than once.	F6
Move to a pane from another pane in the program window (counterclockwise direction).	Shift+F6
When more than one window is open, switch to the next window.	Ctrl+F6
Switch to the previous window.	Ctrl+Shift+F6
Maximize or restore a selected window.	Ctrl+F10
Copy a picture of the screen to the	Print Screen

Clipboard.	
Copy a picture of the selected window to the Clipboard.	Alt+Print Screen

Move around in text or cells

TASK	SHORTCUT
Move one character to the left.	Left Arrow
Move one character to the right.	Right Arrow
Move one line up.	Up Arrow
Move one line down.	Down Arrow
Move one word to the left.	Ctrl+Left Arrow
Move one word to the right.	Ctrl+Right Arrow
Move to the end of a line.	End
Move to the beginning of a line.	Home
Move up one paragraph.	Ctrl+Up Arrow
Move down one paragraph.	Ctrl+Down Arrow
Move to the end of a text box.	Ctrl+End
Move to the beginning of a text box.	Ctrl+Home

Move around in and work in tables

TASK	SHORTCUT
Move to the next cell.	Tab
Move to the preceding cell.	Shift+Tab
Move to the next row.	Down Arrow
Move to the preceding row.	Up Arrow
Insert a tab in a cell.	Ctrl+Tab
Start a new paragraph.	Enter
Add a new row at the	Tab at the end of the

| bottom of the table. | last row |

Access and use actions

TASK	SHORTCUT
Display the menu or message for an action. If more than one action is present, switch to the next action and display its menu or message.	Alt+Shift+F10
Select the next item on the action menu.	Down Arrow
Select the previous item on the action menu.	Up Arrow
Perform the action for the selected item on the action menu.	Enter
Close the action menu or message.	Esc

Use dialog boxes

TASK	SHORTCUT
Move to the next option or option group.	Tab
Move to the previous option or option group.	Shift+Tab
Switch to the next tab in a dialog box.	Ctrl+Tab
Switch to the previous tab in a dialog box.	Ctrl+Shift+Tab
Move between options in an open drop-down list, or between options in a group of options.	Arrow keys
Perform the action assigned	Insert

to the selected button; select or clear the selected check box.	
Open the list if it is closed and move to that option in the list.	First letter of an option in a drop-down list
Select an option; select or clear a check box.	Alt+ the letter underlined in an option
Open a selected drop-down list.	Alt+Down Arrow
Close a selected drop-down list; cancel a command and close a dialog box.	Esc
Perform the action assigned to a default button in a dialog box.	Enter

Use edit boxes within dialog boxes

An edit box is a blank in which you type or paste an entry, such as your user name or the path to a folder.

TASK	SHORTCUT
Move to the beginning of the entry.	Home
Move to the end of the entry.	End
Move one character to the left or right, respectively.	Left Arrow or Right Arrow
Move one word to the left.	Ctrl+Left Arrow
Move one word to the right.	Ctrl+Right Arrow
Select or cancel selection one character to the left.	Shift+Left Arrow

Select or cancel selection one character to the right.	Shift+Right Arrow
Select or cancel selection one word to the left.	Ctrl+Shift+Left Arrow
Select or cancel selection one word to the right.	Ctrl+Shift+Right Arrow
Select from the insertion point to the beginning of the entry.	Shift+Home
Select from the insertion point to the end of the entry.	Shift+End

Basic file management

TASK	SHORTCUT
Open a project file (display the **Open** dialog box).	Ctrl+F12
Open a project file (display the **Open** tab in the Backstage view).	Ctrl+O
Save a project file.	Ctrl+S
Create a new project.	Ctrl+N
Print a file (display the **Print** tab in the Backstage view).	Ctrl+P

Use the Open and Save As dialog boxes

TASK	SHORTCUT
Display the **Open** dialog box.	Ctrl+F12
Display the **Open** tab in the Backstage view.	Ctrl+O
Display the **Save As** dialog box.	F12
Open the selected folder or file.	Enter
Open the folder one level above the	Backspace

open folder.	
Delete the selected folder or file.	Delete
Display a shortcut menu for a selected item such as a folder or file.	Shift+F10
Move forward through options	Tab
Move back through options	Shift+Tab
Open the **Look in** list	F4 or Alt+1

Microsoft Project Shortcuts.

Use a Network Diagram

TASK	SHORTCUT
Move to a different Network Diagram box.	Arrow keys
Add Network Diagram boxes to the selection.	Shift+Arrow keys
Move a Network Diagram box. **Note:** You need to set manual positioning first. Select the box you want to move. Click **Format**, and then click **Layout**. Click **Allow manual box positioning**.	Ctrl+Arrow keys
Move to the top Network Diagram box in the view or project.	Ctrl+Home or Shift+Ctrl+Home
Move to the lowest Network Diagram box in the project.	Ctrl+End or Shift+Ctrl+End
Move to the leftmost Network	Home or

Diagram box in the project.	Shift+Home
Move to the rightmost Network Diagram box in the project.	End or Shift+End
Move up one window height.	Page Up or Shift+Page Up
Move down one window height.	Page Down or Shift+Page Down
Move left one window width.	Ctrl+Page Up or Shift+Ctrl+Page Up
Move right one window width.	Ctrl+Page Down or Shift+Ctrl+Page Down
Select the next field in the Network Diagram box.	Enter or Tab
Select the previous field in the Network Diagram box.	Shift+Enter

Use OfficeArt Objects

Move OfficeArt Shapes

TASK	SHORTCUT
Nudge the shape up, down, right, or left.	Arrow keys
Increase the shape's width by 10%.	Shift+Right Arrow
Decrease the shape's width by 10%.	Shift+Left Arrow
Increase the shape's height by 10%.	Shift+Up Arrow
Decrease the shape's height by 10%.	Shift+Down Arrow

Increase the shape's width by 1%.	Ctrl+Shift+Right Arrow
Decrease the shape's width by 1%.	Ctrl+Shift+Left Arrow
Increase the shape's height by 1%.	Ctrl+Shift+Up Arrow
Decrease the shape's height by 1%.	Ctrl+Shift+Down Arrow
Rotate the shape 15 degrees to the right.	Alt+Right Arrow
Rotate the shape 15 degrees to the left.	Alt+Left Arrow

Select and copy OfficeArt objects and text

TASK	SHORTCUT
Select an object (with text selected inside the object).	Esc
Select an object (with an object selected).	Tab or Shift+Tab until the object you want is selected
Select text within an object (with an object selected).	Enter
Select multiple shapes	Press and hold Ctrl while you click the shapes
Select multiple shapes with text	Press and hold Shift while you click the shapes
Cut selected object.	Ctrl+X
Copy selected object.	Ctrl+C
Paste cut or copied object.	Ctrl+V
Paste special.	Ctrl+Alt+V

Copy formatting only.	Ctrl+Shift+C
Paste formatting only.	Ctrl+Shift+V
Paste special.	Ctrl+Alt+V
Group shapes, pictures, or WordArt.	Ctrl+G after you select the items that you want to group
Ungroup shapes, pictures, or WordArt.	Ctrl+Shift+G after you select the group that you want to ungroup
Undo the last action.	Ctrl+Z
Redo the last action.	Ctrl+Y
Add next object to a multi-selection.	Ctrl+Click
Adds next object to a multi-selection; allows clicking on textbox text to add the textbox to the multi-selection.	Shift+Click

Edit OfficeArt text and textboxes

TASK	SHORTCUT
Collapse selection.	Esc
Select all text.	Ctrl+A
Delete one word to the left.	Ctrl+Backspace
Delete one word to the right.	Ctrl+Delete
Undo.	Ctrl+Z
Redo.	Ctrl+Y
Move one word to the left.	Ctrl+Left Arrow
Move one word to the right.	Ctrl+Right Arrow
Move to the beginning of the line.	Home

Move to the end of the line.	End
Move up one paragraph.	Ctrl+Up Arrow
Move down one paragraph.	Ctrl+Down Arrow
Move to the beginning of the object's text.	Ctrl+Home
Move to the end of the object's text	Ctrl+End

Navigate Views And Windows.

TASK	SHORTCUT
Activate the entry bar to edit text in a field.	F2
Activate the menu bar.	F10 or Alt
Activate the project control menu.	Alt+Hyphen or Alt+Spacebar
Activate the split bar.	Shift+F6
Close the program window.	Alt+F4
Display all filtered tasks or all filtered resources.	F3
Display the **Field Settings** dialog box.	Alt+F3
Open a new window.	Shift+F11
Reduce a selection to a single field.	Shift+Backspace
Reset sort order to ID order and turn off grouping.	Shift+F3
Select a drawing object.	F6
Display task information.	Shift+F2
Display resource information.	Shift+F2
Display assignment	Shift+F2

information.	
Turn on or off the Add To Selection mode.	Shift+F8
Turn on or off Auto Calculate.	Ctrl+F9
Turn on or off the Extend Selection mode.	F8
Move left, right, up, or down to view different pages in the Print Preview window.	Alt+Arrow keys

Outline A Project.

TASK	SHORTCUT
Hide subtasks.	Alt+Shift+Hyphen or Alt+Shift+Minus Sign (minus sign on the numeric keypad)
Indent the selected task.	Alt+Shift+Right Arrow
Show subtasks.	Alt+Shift+ = or Alt+Shift+Plus Sign (plus sign on the numeric keypad)
Show all tasks.	Alt+Shift+* (asterisk on the numeric keypad)
Outdent the selected task.	Alt+Shift+Left Arrow

Select and edit in a dialog box

TASK	SHORTCUT
Move between fields at the bottom of a form.	Arrow keys
Move into tables at the bottom of a form.	Alt+1 (left) or Alt+2 (right)
Move to the next task or	Enter

resource.	
Move to the previous task or resource.	Shift+Enter

Select And Edit In A Sheet View.

Edit in a view

TASK	SHORTCUT
Cancel an entry.	Esc
Clear or reset the selected field.	Ctrl+Delete
Copy the selected data.	Ctrl+C
Cut the selected data.	Ctrl+X
Delete the selected data.	Delete
Delete row that has a selected cell.	Ctrl+Minus Sign (on the numeric keypad)
Fill down.	Ctrl+D
Display the **Find** dialog box.	Ctrl+F or Shift+F5
In the **Find** dialog box, continue to the next instance of the search results.	Shift+F4
Use the **Go To** command (**Edit** menu).	F5
Link tasks.	Ctrl+F2
Paste the copied or cut data.	Ctrl+V
Reduce the selection to one field.	Shift+Backspace
Undo the last action.	Ctrl+Z
Unlink tasks.	Ctrl+Shift+F2

Set the task to manually schedule	Ctrl+Shift+M
Set the task to auto schedule	Ctrl+Shift+A

Move in a view

TASK	SHORTCUT
Move to the beginning of a project (timescale).	Alt+Home
Move to the end of a project (timescale).	Alt+End
Move the timescale left.	Alt+Left Arrow
Move the timescale right.	Alt+Right Arrow
Move to the first field in a row.	Home or Ctrl+Left Arrow
Move to the first row.	Ctrl+Up Arrow
Move to the first field of the first row.	Ctrl+Home
Move to the last field in a row.	End or Ctrl+Right Arrow
Move to the last field of the last row.	Ctrl+End
Move to the last row.	Ctrl+Down Arrow

Move in the side pane

TASK	SHORTCUT
Move focus between the side pane and the view on the right side.	Ctrl+Tab or Ctrl+Shift+Tab
Select different controls in the side pane if focus is in the side	Tab

pane.	
Select or clear check boxes and option buttons if focus is in the side pane.	Spacebar

Select in a view

TASK	SHORTCUT
Extend the selection down one page.	Shift+Page Down
Extend the selection up one page.	Shift+Page Up
Extend the selection down one row.	Shift+Down Arrow
Extend the selection up one row.	Shift+Up Arrow
Extend the selection to the first field in a row.	Shift+Home
Extend the selection to the last field in a row.	Shift+End
Extend the selection to the start of the information.	Ctrl+Shift+Home
Extend the selection to the end of the information.	Ctrl+Shift+End
Extend the selection to the first row.	Ctrl+Shift+Up Arrow
Extend the selection to the last row.	Ctrl+Shift+Down Arrow
Extend the selection to the first field of the first row.	Ctrl+Shift+Home
Extend the selection to the last field of the last row.	Ctrl+Shift+End
Select all rows and columns.	Ctrl+Shift+Spacebar

Select a column.	Ctrl+Spacebar
Select a row.	Shift+Spacebar
Move within a selection down one field.	Enter
Move within a selection up one field.	Shift+Enter
Move within a selection right one field.	Tab
Move within a selection left one field.	Shift+Tab

Select and edit in the entry bar

TASK	SHORTCUT
Accept an entry.	Enter
Cancel an entry.	Esc
Delete one character to the left.	Backspace
Delete one character to the right.	Delete
Delete one word to the right.	Ctrl+Delete
Extend the selection to the end of the text.	Shift+End
Extend the selection to the start of the text.	Shift+Home
Turn on or off Overtype mode.	Insert

Use a timescale

TASK	SHORTCUT
Move the timescale left one page.	Alt+Page Up
Move the timescale right one page.	Alt+Page Down
Move the timescale to	Alt+Home

beginning of the project.	
Move the timescale to end of the project.	Alt+End
Scroll the timescale left.	Alt+Left Arrow
Scroll the timescale right.	Alt+Right Arrow
Show smaller time units.	Ctrl+ / (slash on the numeric keypad)
Show larger time units.	Ctrl+* (asterisk on the numeric keypad)

Customer's Page.

This page is for customers who enjoyed Microsoft Project 2016 Keyboard Shortcuts For Windows.

Dearly beloved customer, please leave a review behind if you enjoyed this book or found it helpful. It will be highly appreciated, thank you.

Other Books By This Publisher.

S/N	Title	Series
Series A: Limits Breaking Quotes.		
1	Discover Your Key Christian Quotes	Limits Breaking Quotes
Series B: Shortcut Matters.		
1	Windows 7 Shortcuts	Shortcut Matters
2	Windows 7 Shortcuts & Tips	Shortcut Matters
3	Windows 8.1 Shortcuts	Shortcut Matters
4	Windows 10 Shortcut Keys	Shortcut Matters
5	Microsoft Office 2007 Keyboard Shortcuts For Windows.	Shortcut Matters
6	Microsoft Office 2010 Shortcuts For Windows.	Shortcut Matters
7	Microsoft Office 2013 Shortcuts For Windows.	Shortcut Matters
Series C: Teach Yourself.		
1	Teach Yourself Computer Fundamentals	Teach Yourself
Series D: For Painless Publishing		
1	Self-Publish it with CreateSpace.	For Painless Publishing
2	Where is my money? Now solved for Kindle and CreateSpace	For Painless Publishing
3	Describe it on Amazon	For Painless Publishing
4	How To Market That Book.	For Painless Publishing